THE ART OF THEATRICAL  MAKE-UP

BY

CAVENDISH MORTON

ILLUSTRATED WITH THIRTY-TWO REPRODUCTIONS
FROM PHOTOGRAPHS OF THE AUTHOR BY HIMSELF

LONDON
ADAM AND CHARLES BLACK
1909

PREFACE

L OOKING back on the method of production of this book, it seems to me not to have been so much a matter of toil as a natural growth. It seems to have produced itself, for my earliest photographs were taken as records of the different characters that I played. These studies, as they were published from time to time in the *Sketch*, *Tatler*, *Playgoer*, and other papers, aroused a certain amount of interest.

Frequent requests from brother actors for me to help them with their make-ups convinced me that my instruction was desired.

As the material accumulated, I constantly heard the suggestion reiterated, " Make a book of it."

A profound interest in psychology, physiognomy, or characterisation, the art of the stage, and photography, has enabled me to study the subject from different standpoints, and to gain an entirely individual impression of it.

Many years spent on the stage in, among others,

Sir Herbert Beerbohm Tree's, Mr. Forbes Robertson's, and Sir Charles Wyndham's companies, the privilege of watching Sir Henry Irving, Sir Herbert, Charles Warner, Franklin McLeay, and M. de Max making up, and, in some instances, hearing their methods of work explained, has supplemented the knowledge gained by my own experience.

CONTENTS

LIST OF ILLUSTRATIONS

.

CHAPTER I

THE ART OF THE STAGE

HOW ephemeral is this art of the stage, how evanescent. Words quickened by the voices of the actors tremble for a moment in the sympathetic atmosphere of the theatre and are then engulfed in silence. This in its turn gives way to newly spoken words. Out of the illustrative gestures and actions of the players are pictures formed which each new phase of the unfolding of the play destroys. Joy gives place to grief, and grief to joy, gentleness to rage, and love to hate.

The passions wax and wane. The scenes fade even as the lantern pictures vanish from the white screen. The curtain rustles down, severing those bonds of sympathy that the play has forged. Actors and audience turn away to pick up the links in their own particular chains of destiny.

How ephemeral, how evanescent.

Yet that universal law of compensation yields its recompense : for no art is more enduring in its influence.

Most men are so profoundly impressed by the drama that the recollection of a performance will abide for years;

1   A

indeed some are so sensitive to its effect that their whole lives are coloured or are even changed by the sensation created by one fine bit of acting.

That the art of the theatre should be so persuasive is in no way strange, for it makes a joint appeal through the portals of two senses simultaneously. The eye and ear alike are charmed.

In this joint appeal lies the very essence of the theatrical. The actor by the heat of his passions fuses picture and poem.

Dumb poetry and petrified graphic art come to life.

Like an electrode the actor stands collecting the currents of dramatic beauty that pervade the world, and discharges them into the tense atmosphere of the theatre.

It is the player's duty not only to lend life to the part that he plays, he should present the character in such a way that the spirit of each member of his audience moves in accord with it. If his appeal is strong it will weld the minds of his individual spectators into a kind of composite intelligence.

I once saw a concave reflector made of small pieces of flat looking glass. These tiny mirrors multiplied the light placed in front a thousandfold.

To the actor a well-crowded theatre should seem just such a reflection. In the mind of each member of his audience, should he, as in a glass, be mirrored.

This unanimity of emotion is brought about by presenting certain physical and mental facts relative to character in such a way that they may be grasped by a number of variously constituted people.

A play is woven of a warp-like plot running from beginning to end of the composition, constituting its chief strength ; and woof-like characterisations which wend their way in and out through the plot binding it together and filling in gaps with the subsidiary interest of nicely contrasted types.

The character as it leaves the playwright's hand is a broadly outlined drawing. The subtleties of manner and expression and those slight but significant inflections of voice are the creation of the actor. He vitalises the lines with his spirit.

I have often thought that the appeal to the brain through the sense of seeing is stronger than that through the sense of hearing. I have been brought to this conclusion by the fact that people are deeply moved by the contemplation of a play in a language that they are totally ignorant of, or by the dumb show of a pantomime.

Is not half the battle won when one perfectly physically realises the character to be impersonated ?

To assist in this half of the conflict this book was written.

CHAPTER II

ON DESIGNING THE CHARACTER

LET us suppose that you have read the play, you know what the plot is about, and the part has been given to you to study. Perhaps the author describes the peculiarities of the character, or it is traditional to make up for the part in a given way. Failing help in either of these directions you must rely upon your own imagination.

Read the part through, trying to think of the character as distinct from yourself. Pretend that you are listening to the words spoken by another. Decide what kind of a man would say such words and behave in such a manner. What are his moral and mental characteristics?

Visualise him, think of him not as an element of the play but as one who on his journey through life has been accidentally involved in the dramatic conflict. Get acquainted with him, try to know something of his past life, for time and experience will have left their marks upon him.

This fiction once designed, the next task is to see how it will fit.

Study yourself with a view to finding out what traits you

4

have in common with the character. Note the qualities that must be accentuated and those that must be subdued.

Alter the character of your face by changing the expression of your mouth and eyes.

Always remember that as little paint should be used as possible, for though it is easy to disguise by a thick mask of pigment, the heavier the make-up the more difficult it is to convey sensitive emotional variations by the changing expression of the face.

If it is possible to arrange your own hair in a way suitable to the character so much the better, for though it may in no way seem more real than a wig it will prove infinitely more comfortable.

I remember before M. de Max played l'Aiglon, he stayed in the house for weeks while his dark locks were slowly dyed a brilliant red. On the night following the production he told me disgustedly that people had criticised his wig.

When you look as much like the part as you possibly can without the aid of artificial disguise, begin to apply nose paste, paint and powder. Obliterate one characteristic and accentuate another. Alter the shape of your nose, paint your eyebrows out and redraw them, altering their form. Change the colour of the skin. Cover eyelashes and lips with paint and note the difference. Put shadows round the eyes, sinister lines running from the nostrils. Wrinkle your face, and where the lines would naturally come apply the paint. Add a roughly shaped beard or moustache of crepe hair if the character demands it.

Stand at a distance from the mirror, study the result. This work is similar to that of the painter when he makes preliminary sketches, it helps to get one's ideas into a concrete form.

It should be done over and over again until the character is perfectly developed.

If a wig is required, discuss it with the best wig-maker that you can find. Should you be able to draw supply him with a rough sketch. Failing this you will probably be able to find an illustration or an engraving which, though it may not be exactly what you want, will help you to explain your idea.

I have made a large collection of different engravings of interesting types, and the work of the old caricaturists I have found very suggestive.

Visit the wig-maker two or three times before the wig is completed, it will then be made under your direct supervision and will probably be more successful in every way.

Remember that the character of a face depends on three elemental qualities, form, colour and expression. The first two are almost constant, the third is susceptible to perpetual change.

The grave, the gay, the ascetic, the debauched, the æsthetic, the philistine, the spiritual and the material, each will have his distinguishing colour and form. The expression will depend much on the various moods portrayed during the action of the play.

Make the characterisation as definite as possible, for the

size of the stage demands a certain breadth of treatment. Do not forget the distant patron of the pit and gallery, for though his monetary contribution is humble he atones for this by the warmth of his enthusiasm.

If the result of these preliminary efforts seem discouraging, remember a good wig and suitable costume will help materially.

CHAPTER III

THE ILLUSTRATIONS

IN making all the pictures in the book studies of my own head I was actuated by a number of reasons. The first and most important of which was the possibility of showing what a wide variety of distinctive types could be realised with the help of make-up by one man.

If the book had been illustrated by a number of pictures of various actors, the student would have had to make in each instance certain allowances for the individuality of each performer.

My desire was to present only one face under different disguises.

I was also influenced by the fact that my own face was the one that was ever nearest to my hand—the one I was most familiar with, and also the one that I could take the greatest number of liberties with.

Another reason was, that as the photographer who was to produce the prints, I could always depend upon the attendance of the model. I was sure that I could always induce myself to patiently pose before my own camera.

The taking of the photographs has been fraught with

considerable difficulty. The playing of the dual *rôle* of actor and photographer seems to have cultivated two distinct personalities—personalities who I am sure felt the liveliest interest one for the other; in fact nothing ever came between us but the camera.

I am moved less by pride than by a desire for sympathy when I say that single-handed I did every detail of the work. Sometimes it was necessary to photograph one character nine times over before a suitable negative was obtained.

Can you imagine the feelings of Othello or King Lear who, after having worked up to the most intense moment of the play, paused rigidly before the camera, that it might do the worst, then on retiring to the dim ruby light of the dark room, still made up remember, to wrestle with the difficulties of development, found that when the negative was finished it was a failure and would have to be done again.

I feel a great debt of gratitude to Sir Herbert Beerbohm Tree, Mr. Charles Warner, Mr. R. G. Knowles, Mr. Carton, More-Park, and many other actors and painters who have unfailingly encouraged me with the bounty of their interest and their expressions of willingness to assist me with the work.

I can best express the admiration I feel for the work of my friend M. Gustav by calling attention to the perfection of the wigs that appear in the following prints. I believe that he has brought wig-making to a pitch never realised before. Much of the effectiveness of my impersonations is in no small measure due to his sympathy and skill.

B

I selected for my illustrations, in most cases extreme types; sometimes presented in a more or less exaggerated manner. I felt that thus I might cover a wide area and make the book the more suggestive.

The student will find but little difficulty in modifying a character, or if he requires only certain features, in selecting them. Or he may combine certain peculiarities of one make-up with the peculiarities of another, and thus produce an additional type.

Many of the characters slightly modified will prove valuable as studies for modern personalities.

With the exception of those prints where the make-up is shown in progressive stages I have striven to exhibit the character under the stress of one of the most emotional moments of the play, illuminated in a manner that would be desirable to its stage presentation.

I have done this because I felt that a character was essentially a medium of emotional expression, and that by presenting them in this way the sensitiveness and flexibility of the characterisation might be better realised.

Or in other words, that the disguise in no way impaired the ability to show a great variety of facial expressions.

When I originally contemplated the work I feared that it would be difficult to get a sufficient number of contrasted types to make the book interesting, but I found, once under way, there was literally no end to the quaint creatures that clamoured to be noticed. It became a hard matter to select, and I have only introduced to the public a few of the odd personalities I have grown so intimately acquainted with. Each has been to me a living creature, who was able to let me see the world from his peculiar standpoint.

I had such an impulse in the work, that at one time I felt that I should not be able to rest until I had exhausted all human creation. Aye, perhaps not even then, but would have to wend my way through all the animal kingdom, till I ended up by trying to make myself look like inanimate things such as icebergs or lumps of coal.

The undertaking has not been altogether free from pathetic associations. It was done during the period of my father's last illness, and the pleasure that he derived from the visit of each new character cheered, I am sure, his last hours on earth.

CHAPTER IV

THE MATERIAL

WHEN we consider the materials, we realise that the art of make-up is more or less allied to the art of the painter; although the kinship may not be of a very intimate character. It resembles in many particulars coloured statuary, with this great difference, that in the case of the actor the statue is alive.

If the student were to have a bust of himself accurately modelled by a sculptor and were to apply the various articles of make-up to it, he would get almost precisely the same effects that he would get from his own face, minus, of course, the ability to change its expression.

I have such a bust, and I find that I can do much of my experimenting upon my dumb counterpart without either its skin or temper ever resenting the torture. Though I do not think that many will care to follow my example in this particular I offer the suggestion as being of some value.

Among the men who paint pictures you rarely find two who use exactly similar materials, or work in precisely similar ways, in fact methods of work and the tools used

12

depend largely upon individual differences of temperament. So in the following pages I trust that it may be felt that I am suggesting in a more or less stimulating way, and that I am not dogmatising.

If we again compare it with painting we shall find that we get the most valuable hints from that branch which is known as the impressionist school.

The enormous size of the proscenium, which is really only the frame of our canvas, and the distance which is ever between the spectator and the stage, demand great breadth of treatment.

I have known an actor to strive for almost the same delicacy of detail as would be found in a highly finished portrait, and although the illusion from the front of the house was not positively wrong, much of his work was never realised ; in fact with one quarter the effort he could have produced a result which would have been infinitely more telling.

Doubtless many who read this book will have had a wide experience in making up, and will have cultivated pre-ferences for one selection of materials or another. To them I submit my method and its results. To the man who comes to the subject with an absolutely unbiassed mind, I would suggest that he begin his work with a very limited range of colours, for in this way he will materially simplify the problem.

The following is a list of the grease-paints that may be purchased from any dealer in make-up :

No. 1, lightest flesh colour; 1½, slightly darker; 2, pale;

2½, medium ; 3, slightly darker; 3½, sunburnt; 4, a ruddy deep flesh colour ; 5, bright yellow; 5½, dark; 6, darker yellow ; 7, brown ; 8, Armenian bole; 9, dark sunburn ; 10, brown; 11, burnt umber; 12, black ; 13, reddish brown ; 14, chocolate; 15, brick red; 16, dark brown ; 20, white ; carmine 1, 2 and 3.

Of these the colours that prove most valuable in my hands are 2½, 3, 10-13, yellow, white and black, and the following lining sticks ; light blue, dark blue, yellow, lake brown, and carmine 2.

I never use any one of these colours in its crude state, but by blending produce the exact shade that I deem desirable.

The palm of the left hand proves an admirable palette ; its heat readily melting the paint.

A draughtsman's stub may be used for putting in the wrinkles and softening the shadows, but I have found the most suitable instrument for this work is a small modelling tool such as is used for modelling in wax. It has one end slightly curved and then brought to a knife-like edge. It is not only valuable for applying colours, but enables one to deftly finish the shaping of nose-paste.

A small quantity of nose-paste, or, what I have found work better, toupee paste, will be required. A bottle of spirit gum for applying false beards and moustaches. Crepe hair of various colours. Powders I mix for myself that I may get a tint to match any given make-up. The foundation of this is of a light pink to which I add a little Armenian bole and yellow. Powders, however, of various hues may be bought which will save the trouble of mixing. A good powder puff, a box of dry rouge, a hare's-foot, a pair of scissors and a comb. Vaseline, cold-cream, cocoa butter, or my preference, olive oil, for removing the make-up will complete the outfit.

Various elaborate make-up boxes of tin are on the market, but any small box will answer. The one that always accompanies me on my travels is an antique case of oak, and was no doubt used for generations as a receptacle for jewels. It has but one tray, which has sufficient space for the reception of the various paints. The lower part is reserved for crepe hair, powder and the other requisites.

CHAPTER V

ON APPLYING THE MATERIAL

THE actual work of making up must fall under the two headings of Form and Colour. We will consider first

COLOUR

The colour of a man's skin, or his complexion, may be indicative of his nationality or race. For example, consider the distinctive colourings of the English, Italians, Japanese, Indians, or Africans. It may suggest his age. For youth has its own peculiar freshness; the healthy meridian of life is florid, while pallor comes with old age. We may also vividly realise temperament from the tint of the skin. The sad, the morbid, and the mean are usually sallow; the happy and generous, brilliantly hued. Trades and professions also dye their followers to their liking. The monk is bleached in the cloister, the soldier or sailor is browned by the sun and wind.

Having decided on the complexion that will be characteristic of a given part, we mix and apply the paint.

16

Are we to present an English soldier back from a foreign campaign No. 3 grease-paint, mixed with a little 13, will yield exactly the sunburnt hue that we desire. We must remember though that the upper part of the forehead has been protected from the sun's rays by his helmet, and so a distinct line of light flesh will remain. No. 2½ will do for this.

A mixture of 2½, yellow and a little brown will provide suitable pallidness. Such as we might imagine would be characteristic of the miser.

We cover the face with No. 3, and then deepening the hue of some more No. 3 on our palm with a little lake and carmine, and working this over the face in fleck-like blotches, we shall obtain the floridness of the man who drinks, or perhaps even eats too much.

I give these few examples to show the importance of first deciding what the actual complexion of the character shall be. This paint, which is spread all over the face is called the groundwork.

By a suitable application of colour, in the way of shadows and of high lights, we can give the illusion of a different form of feature or of face.

Let it always be remembered that the shadow is almost invariably of a similar colour to the rest of the face, only darker. This darkening may be done with brown, lake, or blue. For example, if the prevailing tone of the skin is 2½ mixed with yellow and a brown, the same mixture with considerably more brown added to it will give us exactly the pigment we require for the shadows and

c

wrinkles, remembering always that the depth of the wrinkles will be darkest. The same mixture, lightened with additional yellow and white until it is very pale indeed, will give the high lights.

The shadows round the eyes of the sickly and in their sunken cheeks will be bluish. A little lake and blue mixed with the groundwork will do for this.

Always strive to keep the colouring as light and brilliant as possible; only thus may a dirty appearance be avoided.

Finish up the make-up with plenty of powder of a colour that suits that of the groundwork.

CHAPTER VI

FORM

THE variation of form that may be suggested by painted high lights and shadows is effective enough when the full face is observed. For instance an almost white line on the bridge of the nose seems to give this feature additional prominence when the actor looks directly toward you, but on getting a view of his profile this illusion disappears, in fact the true shape of the nose is realised.

If it is desirable to really alter the shape of a feature, a face, or even the entire head, another method must be used.

The simplest and most popular is the application of nose paste, or what I personally prefer toupee paste. A sufficient quantity of this material is taken and kneaded into a soft mass. To do this it is sometimes necessary to warm it slightly. It is formed roughly into the shape desired and then stuck to the skin. Some make its adhesion more certain by applying a small quantity of spirit gum to the skin first. I have found it better to melt the surface of the paste in the heat of a candle before placing it into position. When the paste has adhered to the skin a little grease applied to it with the fingers will facilitate the subsequent shaping. The modelling should be carefully finished with the fingers and a modelling tool until no juncture is observable. In fact it should seem to be part of the face. Plenty of groundwork spread all over the actual flesh and the parts that have been built out brings the whole face into accord.

The nose paste can be used for altering the shape of the nose either by making the bridge more prominent, the end longer, and this increase in its length may be made in any direction either up or down. The nostrils fuller, in fact, the whole nose may be covered, and its shape and size entirely changed.

In a similar way the prominence of the forehead and of the cheek bones may be built out and additions may also be made to the chin.

It is well to remember that all such distinctive features are due to the shape of the underlying bony structure of the skull, and when we desire to alter the shape we must do it in such a way that all the laws of anatomy are not ignored.

The paste may also be used for imitating unpleasant growths such as warts and moles.

The entire outline of the head may be altered by the shape of the wig. On deciding what this alteration shall be it is simplest to think of it as having roughly a geo-metrical form. A head may be round, square, or oblong, and this distinctive form is noticeable when either the full face or profile is observed.

When ordering the wig even a very rough sketch will prove of great assistance to the wig-maker.

The beard is also a great help in changing the shape of the face. The chin may be strengthened or modified by a suitable arrangement of the hair.

A great double chin of padded silk is sometimes worn round the neck, but this is only convincing when the chin is slightly bearded.

The foregoing alterations have almost all been in the shape of additions to the features. We will now consider how modifications may be made.

The first time that I played the part of a negro I found that I should not be able to imitate the flattened nose of the race unless I used some method to depress my own very prominent organ. I found that by holding the tip of my nose down with my finger I very nearly got the illusion I required. I next took a piece of strong sewing silk, and first protecting the skin of my nose with a piece of kid, passed the silk over this, and tying this at the back of my head got exactly what I required. Then building the nostrils out with nose paste and covering it all with dark grease paint I look sufficiently negroid to deceive a native.

The nose may be given a very decided upward tilt by passing a similar thread under the end of it. This thread is then joined to the upper part of the wig.

At a short distance these threads are not noticeable.

CHAPTER VII

PREPARING THE MAKE-UP

IN adopting the following method in preparing to make-up, I have been actuated by a desire to preserve the health of my body, and as far as possible the wholesomeness of my skin.

Acting is sometimes such violent physical exercise that precautions should be taken against catching cold. Therefore on entering my dressing-room I change my underclothing.

I next put on tights or any lower garment that part demands. To free the face from any dust that might be rubbed into the pores by the process of making-up I wash with pure Castile soap and warm water. Then thoroughly dry the skin with a soft towel.

While making-up I wear a cotton dressing-gown.

My dressing-table has a large mirror flanked by two electric lights. On this table the grease paints, wig and other materials that I require for a given make-up are arranged.

First a little oil is thoroughly rubbed into the skin· filling the pores and keeping them from being clogged with the paint.

I next build up with nose-paste any features that require additional relief. Then the face, neck and ears are covered with a thin layer of 2½ grease paint. This is done that all inequalities of colour may be eliminated, and enables one to subsequently get a smooth, clean groundwork, no matter what colour is desired.

I put on my wig, taking care that the join is invisibly blended. The face, neck and ears are then covered with a suitable groundwork that I mix on the palm of my hand. The broad shadows are next introduced, such as sunken cheeks, temples, and shadows round the eyes.

The accentuation, with smaller shadows, of the mouth and eyes is the next work. Wrinkles are added, care being taken that they are placed at places that nature would select. This may be discovered by actually wrinkling the face and observing where the lines fall. High lights are then applied.

If a beard or moustache is to be worn, carefully remove the paint with a clean towel from the part that will be covered by the false hair and apply a little spirit gum to the clean skin. Adjust the beard and hold it until it adheres thoroughly. Always blend the beard with the cheeks with loosely-combed crepe hair as this will help the naturalness of the appearance. Powder the face. The eyelashes are darkened by drawing a thin line along the edges of the lids. This I do with an orange stick dipped in melted paint. The eyebrows are then drawn in. The make-up is finished by colouring the lips.

I occasionally walk back from the mirror that I may get an impression such as a distant spectator might receive.

The hands and arms are made up if the character demands it.

The dressing is completed and I step in front of a full-length mirror for a final inspection prior to going upon the stage.

What the precise impression is that I make upon my audience I cannot say, I only know that in many character parts I have been unable to recognise myself.

The time that it takes to make-up must of course vary with the complexity of the characterisation. At dress-rehearsals when I make-up for character for the first time I allow myself one hour and a half, but this when I get more experienced with the part is sometimes reduced to half an hour. The hurry that this necessitates is nerve-racking both for actor and dresser and becomes a race with the call-boy. "Half an hour please," he shouts, his voice echoing up the stairs. Then you begin to work furiously. When what seems only a few minutes gone by, his second warning, "A quarter of an hour, please," is heard. Then you increase your speed. When the boy calls "Overture," if you are not almost dressed you tell your dresser with more decision than taste that you know that you will be off. "First-act beginners" means a bad-tempered rush for the stage, and the struggle with final buttons on your way. Once upon the stage you almost invariably find that you have a few minutes in which to regain your breath. Then, warmed by the glare of the footlights, you forget that you have ever hurried in your life. In fact, if you are a good actor you forget everything but the part you play.

CHAPTER VIII

ON REMOVING THE MAKE-UP

AT the conclusion of the play you retire to your dressing-room, flushed, I hope, with success. To resume your real self is a matter of little difficulty, and yet it may be helpful to have a method suggested.

Begin by removing parts of the clothing, as it unquestionably would be soiled in the dirty process of removing the make-up.

First take off the wig, next the moustache, then the beard; carefully remove the false nose, or any other modelling in relief, for if they are preserved with care they may be used repeatedly. Next, with a small quantity of oil, or any other grease that may be preferred, soften the grease-paint slightly and remove it with a towel. This first cleansing will only remove part of the colour, in fact, the treatment with oil must be repeated two or three times before every trace of paint has disappeared. When this has been achieved, wash thoroughly with warm water and pure Castile soap; dry the face, taking care that every vestige of paint has been removed.

If the weather is cold, a little cold cream rubbed into the skin, which is then slightly powdered, will protect it.

CHAPTER IX

IN CONCLUSION

PERHAPS no other calling is as fascinating as that of the stage. Are we not happiest when we are least mindful of ourselves, and does not absolute self-forgetfulness come with a complete realisation of a personality that is foreign to us? Plus this is the pleasure to be derived from the knowledge of the strength possessed which enables the swaying of multitudes by sympathy.

To the born actor his art is a delightful pastime. All his observations of art and life augment his knowledge of character and his ability to portray emotion.

The less gifted should study perpetually. The world is full of odd volumes in strange and interesting bindings. To the student of make-up the binding is of no less interest than the matter within.

Try to store vivid recollections of the distinctive types; collect caricatures and prints; they will be most suggestive and helpful.

If you possess even only a slight talent for drawing, cultivate it assiduously, for it is obvious that the actor who can draw will be able to make-up better than the one who cannot.

Visit picture galleries and turn them into museums of types. I know of no other gallery that interests me so much as the National Portrait Gallery. When I am in London I try to visit it at least once a week. There I realise what each one of a legion of distinguished men looked like.

If a play revives some period of history, try to see some of the pictures of the greatest painters of that day, or at least get reproductions of their work. Perhaps the very man that you require is standing in some dim canvas only waiting for you to make him live again.

Remember that each period of history had its distinctive types. Think of the people of Gainsborough, of Velasquez, the portraits of Holbein and of Dürer.

If you are to present a man of an alien race, try and give him his national peculiarities without offering his country the insult of burlesquing them. I think it is a sign of decadence of our stage that we strive to heap ridicule on almost every type that is not a product of our own land.

If any of the dark races are to be presented, such as Africans, Red Indians, or Japanese, trustworthy photographs may be bought which will prove an admirable guide.

If you are to portray a well-known historical character, read everything you can about the man. Perhaps you will have the fortune to come across a detailed description by one of his intimate friends.

If the man you represent follows any particular trade or calling, try to get acquainted with some such men. Take, for example, a foundry hand. Get permission to visit a foundry; go there several times, till the significance of the work is borne home to you. You will eventually realise not only what the men look like, but the way they feel, and will be able to suggest the way in which they toil. Tinker, tailor, soldier, sailor, rich man, poor man, beggarman, thief. What a drama of characterisation the line conveys; each is stamped with his trade or condition.

Go again and again to life; let your body and brain reflect it. Make your types actual.

A Parliament, a Court, a ward of a hospital, with its quiet doctor going from bed to bed. The deck of the steamer, the interior of a bus—they each become a school where valuable lessons may be learnt.

Unless you suffer from very definite physical or vocal limitations, strive not to get grooved in your work. Do not repeat yourself over and over again in each new part that you play.

Remember that the number of types in the world is infinite; that the playwright is always striving to present to the public some new character.

Ever add to your knowledge, and recollect that work is life's great recompense. Thank God your toil is endless.

ILLUSTRATIONS

KING LEAR

Blow, winds, and crack your cheeks! rage! blow!
You cataracts, and hurricanoes, spout
Till you have drench'd our steeples, drown'd the cocks!
You sulphurous and thought-executing fires,
Vaunt couriers to oak-cleaving thunder-bolts,
Singe my white head!   And thou, all shaking thunder,
Strike flat the thick rotundity o' the world!
Crack nature's moulds, all germes spill at once
That make ingrateful man!

38

KING LEAR

This old man torn to rags by a tempest of emotion, on the ultimate boundary of life, is obviously difficult to portray ; tenderness and rage, madness and dignity, must all be shown. He is pent, baffled, and buffeted by things physical and mental for a while. Then there is the hurried decay of body and of brain.

In Fig. 1 observe that the nose has been slightly built up. This is done to give added dignity to the face. For the great weight of beard and hair would tend to make the nose look smaller than it really is. After the nose has been built up the wig is put on that the position of the join may be indicated, also what parts of the natural hair must be treated with white paint. The groundwork is laid on : this should be of 2½ yellow and a little brown. The shadows round the eyes are of groundwork mixed with blue. The wrinkles are of groundwork mixed with additional brown and lake. The temples should be shadowed with this colour.

Find out where the wrinkles would come by pursing up the face. Use as many as possible to suggest extreme old age, being always mindful that the intentions of nature are not ignored. Be careful that the lines on the face are not drawn in too decisive a manner, as at a distance they seem much stronger than they really are. The modelling tool is most suitable for the drawing and the subsequent modification of the wrinkles. It may be also used for applying the more delicate high lights. Each wrinkle should be accentuated with a light just above it. Fig. 2 shows the make-up at a stage when it is ready for the addition of the moustache and beard. Observe the whitened hair just above the temples. This is done with white grease paint.

Fig. 3 shows the beard in position. A tape goes over the head to partly support its weight, and it is secured with spirit gum. Note the blending of the left cheek and beard with crepe hair, also how half the chin is covered, observe how the character of the face is altered by the bushy eyebrow. Fig. 4 shows the make-up almost complete and ready for the wig to be put on. Put the wig on, carefully blending the join. Accentuate wrinkles and shadows here and there. Powder and treat the eyelashes with white paint.

DON QUIXOTE

Fantastic to the point of madness, of romantic daring. Simple and kind ; and above all a nobleman of great dignity.

I have chosen this extreme make-up as a foil to the Falstaff.

Falstaff is a creature of utter coarseness. Quixote as a singularly imaginative man is one of extraordinary sensitiveness.

The chief effort was to make the face as long and as thin as possible.

First compare the four progressive prints. See how much longer the head is in Fig. 4 than in Fig. 1. As the four photographs are taken to exactly the same scale it is possible to accurately measure with a draughtsman's compass the additions that have been made to the chin and forehead. It will be found that the head has been increased by one third.

First the nose is built up with paste. By giving it a very pronounced hook it is decidedly lengthened and thus made to accord better with the new proportions of the face.

The prominences of the forehead and cheek bones are next accentuated with nose-paste (Fig. 1).

The wig is placed in position and the forehead made up with a ground work of $2\frac{1}{2}$, yellow, and 13, a flesh colour that should suggest parchment. The wig is then removed until the make-up is almost finished. This keeps it from becoming soiled.

Covering the face with groundwork is the next step. A sunken appearance is given to the eyes by painting round them with brown. Shadows are worked into the cheeks. Lines are drawn from the inner corners of the eyes down on to the cheeks. Similar lines are indicated at either side of the nose. A broad perpendicular stripe from the nose to the top of the forehead, and the temples are darkened.

40

44

Yellowish high lights are placed on the forehead at either side of the central shadow and round the temples in such a way that their depth is accentuated.

High lights on the cheek bones and above the various wrinkles make the face more vigorous.

The false eyebrows, the moustache and beard are gummed in position. The beard is blended with loosely combed crepe hair which is afterward trimmed.

The wig is again put on the shadows and high lights carried up with the false forehead.

Yellowish powder is next dusted all over the face. Colour similar to the wig and beard is applied to the eyelashes. The lips are painted with a colour that should not be too dark.

FALSTAFF

If I were sawed into quantities, I should make four dozen of such
bearded hermit's staves as Master Shallow. It is a wonderful thing to
see the semblable coherence of his men's spirits and his. They, by
observing of him, do bear themselves like foolish justices; he, by convers-
ing with them, is turned into a justice-like serving-man. Their spirits
are so married in conjunction with the participation of society, that they
flock together in consent, like so many wild geese. If I had a suit to
Master Shallow, I would humour his men, with the imputation of being
near their master; if to his men, I would curry with Master Shallow
that no man could better command his servants. It is certain that
either wise bearing or ignorant carriage is caught, as men take diseases,
one of another; therefore, let men take heed of their company. I will
devise matter enough out of this Shallow, to keep Prince Harry in con-
tinual laughter the wearing-out of six fashions, which is four terms, or
two actions, and he shall laugh without intervallums. O, it is much,
that a lie, with a slight oath, and a jest, with a sad brow, will do with
a fellow that never had the ache in his shoulders! O, you shall see him
laugh, till his face be like a wet cloak ill laid up.

47

FALSTAFF

A VOLCANO of carnality capped by a head that seems red hot with fleshly passions.

Of all the examples in the book this is the most exaggerated.

In exaggerating to a point of almost buffoonery it has been my wish to show to what extremes make-up could be carried—extremes that should usually be avoided.

The chief intention was to give great additional breadth to the head and face, as opposed to the Don Quixote, in which case the head has been lengthened as much as possible.

What this additional breadth amounts to may be realised by referring to Fig. 1 of the progressive prints.

In Fig. 2 the wig is shown with the silk joined to it from which the cheeks and double chin are to be formed. With spirit gum the edges of the silk are joined round the eyes, mouth and nose. Next the cheeks and chin are padded, and the drawstring at the lower edge of the silk is tightened (see Fig. 3).

A large nose of nose-paste is formed (Fig. 4).

Pouches of nose paste are placed beneath the eyes and these are blended with the false cheeks, effectually covering the joins.

A groundwork of No. 3 grease paint made deeper with yellow, carmine, and a little lake is applied evenly all over the face, or perhaps it would be better to call it a mask. This will bring its various elements into accord.

Blotches of carmine mixed with a little yellow are dabbed on the nose and cheeks. High lights of white mixed with a little yellow are placed on the forehead, on the pouches under the eyes, and on the cheeks. Blend these with the groundwork carefully.

The beard and moustache are so placed that the actual outlines of the cheeks are lost. The beard is blended into the cheeks with crepe hair.

The eyelashes are coloured with reddish yellow making them seem smaller.

51

SHYLOCK

SHYLOCK. I am bid forth to supper, Jessica :
There are my keys.   But wherefore should I go ?
I am not bid for love ; they flatter me :
But yet I'll go in hate, to feed upon
The Prodigal Christian.   Jessica, my girl,
Look to my house.   I am right loth to go :
There is some ill a-brewing towards my rest,
For I did dream of money-bags to-night.

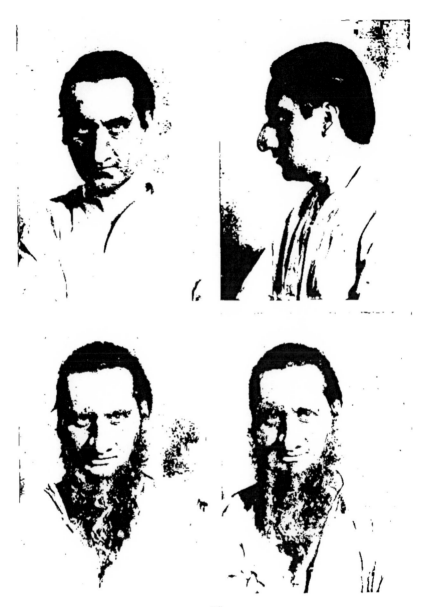

SHYLOCK

A DIGNIFIED figure really, but under the lash of persecution disclosing the evil qualities of revengefulness and craft. Strong, cruel, and resentful.

The nose is built with nose-paste and carefully modelled after it is joined. In the progressive prints, Figs. 1 and 2, two views are given of it.

The groundwork is of No. 3 yellow, a little lake, brown, and 13. Before this is applied to the face, the wig is put on; but after the spreading of the groundwork it is again removed, that it may not be soiled during the subsequent stages of the make-up.

The colour for the shadows and wrinkles is formed of the groundwork with brown and lake added. The cavities of the eyes should be strengthened with this. Deep grooves are painted from the corners of the nose, a sunken appearance given to the temples, and crows' feet drawn from the eyes.

The high lights come above the wrinkles; and are placed on the most prominent parts of the forehead.

The beard, which is of a mixture of black, deep red, and grey hair, is next gummed into position, taking care that no grease paint is on any part of the face to which the gum is to be applied. (See Fig. 3.)

In Fig. 4 the blending of the beard with the cheek is shown, also the placing of half the moustache and a false eyebrow. Observe the small piece of crepe hair that is placed just under the lower lip.

The wig is again put on and carefully blended with the forehead.

A rather deep reddish powder is suitable for the make-up. The lips are coloured with carmine and lake mixed.

G

HAMLET

A MIRROR of emotions. The mouthpiece of protesting souls. A creature of sensitiveness absolute. His face must express almost the entire range of the passions. Very pale, studious, of great mental strength and refinement.

Groundwork $2\frac{1}{2}$, a little yellow and a very small quantity of brown.

Flesh colour that should vaguely suggest ivory. A little white rubbed on to the most prominent parts of the forehead adds intellectuality to the head.

The shadows which should be of the groundwork deepened with brown are so arranged that they intensify the sensitiveness of the face. They are used under the brows to give soulfulness to the eyes and to make the forehead seem more prominent. A line is drawn round the upper part of the nostrils to give delicacy to the drawing of the nose. The darkening of the division of the upper lip and of the cleft chin makes the face seem thinner. The shadows on the temples and on the cheeks also help this illusion.

Cream-coloured powder is applied to the face and neck.

The eyebrows are carefully drawn with brown in a wide clear arch and are afterward lightly combed.

The eyelashes are strengthened by drawing a black line along the edges and this line is carried a little way out at the outer corner of the eyes. A tiny spot of carmine at the inner corner by the tear-bag lends lustre to the eye.

The lips nobly drawn in carmine give passion to the mouth.

The hair is of crisp clean curls which suggests vigour and alertness.

Hamlet when impersonated by fair men has usually been played in a fair make-up, and this example is worth following. The subtle natural peculiarities of a fair face make a dark make-up unsuitable to it and *vice versâ*.

For a fair make-up the same advice should be followed, leaving all the brown and nearly all the yellow out of the groundwork, and finishing with rouge. The make-up should be much brighter and the wig of flaxen.

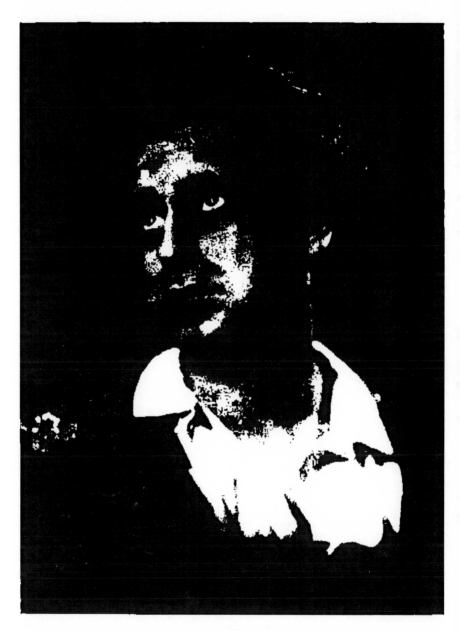

61

HAMLET

The time is out of joint; O cursed spite,
That ever I was born to set it right!

*   *   *

HAMLET (Second Print)

Polonius. * * * What do you read, my lord?

Hamlet. Words, words, words!

Polonius. What is the matter, my lord?

Hamlet. Between who?

Polonius. I mean, the matter that you read, my lord.

Hamlet. Slanders sir; for the satirical rogue says here that old men have grey beards; that their faces are wrinkled; their eyes purging thick amber, and plum-tree gum; and that they have a plentiful lack of wit, together with most weak hams: all of which, sir, though I most powerfully and potently believe, yet I hold it not honesty to have it thus set down; for yourself, sir, shall be as old as I am, if, like a crab, you could go backward.

IAGO

THE personification of cunningness, craft and deceit. A brilliant mind and an utterly corrupted spirit. One that enjoys to contemplate and to study mental suffering.

Pale skin, dark brown hair, and a reddish beard.

Observe the building of the nose. Its bridge runs in an uninterrupted line up to the forehead.

Note the deep shadow of the temples and the manner of colouring the cheeks.

The drooping moustache gives the face a singularly sinister expression.

The beard is of crepe hair and is so arranged that it gives the skin a goatlike appearance.

See instruction for the making of beards.

OTHELLO

OF great natural dignity, simple and loyal. Driven to irresistibly follow an impulse when it has once seized his mind. Tortured to distraction by Iago. All the primitive savagery of his race is manifested.

The nose is first depressed by crossing it near the tip with a silk thread which is tied at the back of the head. A small piece of kid is placed under the thread, thus keeping from coming into contact with the skin. The nostrils are built out until the nose has a Moorish appearance.

The face is first covered with $2\frac{1}{2}$ and subsequently with a mixture of Nos. 10 and 13.

The colouring is made much stronger round the eyes.

High lights are faintly suggested on the forehead and on the cheek bones.

The beard, which had better be of crepe hair, should be so applied that the flesh shows through.

Reddish brown powder is used, and the make-up is finished by painting strong black lines on the edges of the eyelids. The eyebrows are also of black. The lips are No. 13 with a little carmine added.

Ear-rings and a turban help the make-up.

OTHELLO AND IAGO

IAGO. I will in Cassio's lodging lose this napkin,
And let him find it. Trifles, light as air,
Are to the jealous, confirmations strong
As proofs of holy writ. This may do something.
The Moor already changes with my poison:
Dangerous conceits are, in their natures, poisons,
Which, at the first, are scarce found to distaste;
But, with a little act upon the blood,
Burn like the mines of sulphur.—I did say so:—

Enter OTHELLO.

Look, where he comes! Not poppy, nor mandragora,
Nor all the drowsy syrups of the world,
Shall ever medicine thee to that sweet sleep,
Which thou ow'dst yesterday.

    OTHELLO. Ha! ha! false to me? To me?

    IAGO. Why, how now, general? no more of that.

    OTHELLO. Avaunt! be gone! thou hast set me on the rack—
I swear, 'tis better to be much abus'd,
Than but to know't a little.

    IAGO.   How now, my lord?

    OTHELLO. What sense had I of her stolen hours of lust?
I saw't not, thought it not, it harm'd not me:
I slept the next night well, was free and merry;
I found not Cassio's kisses on her lips:
He that is robb'd, not wanting what is stolen,
Let him not know't, and he's not robb'd at all.

    IAGO. I am sorry to hear this.

70

OTHELLO. I had been happy, if the general camp,
Pioneers and all, had tasted her sweet body,
So I had nothing known : O now, for ever,
Farewell, the tranquil mind : farewell content !
Farewell the plumed troop, and the big wars,
That make ambition virtue ! O, farewell !
Farewell the neighing steed, and the shrill trump,
The spirit-stirring drum, the ear-piercing fife,
The royal banner ; and all quality,
Pride, pomp, and circumstance of glorious war !
And O, you mortal engines, whose rude throats
The immortal Jove's dread clamours counterfeit,
Farewell ! Othello's occupation's gone !

    IAGO. Is't possible, my lord ?

    OTHELLO. Villain, be sure thou prove my love a whore :
Be sure of it ; give me the ocular proof ;

                              [*Taking him by the throat.*
Or, by the worth of mine eternal soul,
Thou had'st been better have been born a dog,
Than answer my wak'd wrath.

    IAGO.   Is't come to this ?

    OTHELLO. Make me to see't, or, at the least, so prove it,
That the probation bear no hinge nor loop,
To hang a doubt on ; or woe upon thy life !

    IAGO. My noble lord,—

    OTHELLO. If thou dost slander her, and torture me,
Never pray more ; abandon all remorse :
On horror's head, horrors accumulate :
Do deeds to make heaven weep, all earth amaz'd,
For nothing canst thou to damnation add,
Greater than that.

    IAGO.   O grace ! O heaven forgive me !
Are you a man ? have you a soul or sense ?
God be wi' you ; take mine office. O wretched fool,
That liv'st to make thine honesty a vice !
O monstrous world ! Take note, take note, O world !
To be direct and honest is not safe.

I thank you for this profit ; and, from hence,
I'll love no friend, sith love breeds such offence.

OTHELLO. Nay, stay :—Thou should'st be honest.

IAGO. I should be wise ; for honesty's a fool,
And loses that it works for.

OTHELLO. By the world,
I think my wife be honest, and think, she is not.
I think that thou art just and think thou art not.
I'll have some proof: Her name, that was as fresh
As Dian's visage, is now begrim'd and black
As mine own face. If there be cords, or knives,
Poison, or fire, or suffocating streams,
I'll not endure it. Would I were satisfied !

IAGO. I see, sir, you are eaten up with passion ;
I do repent me, that I put it to you.
You would be satisfied ?

OTHELLO. Would ! nay, I will.

IAGO. And may : But, how ? how satisfied, my lord ?
Would you, the supervisor grossly gape on ?
Behold her tupp'd ?

OTHELLO. Death and damnation ! O !

IAGO. It were a tedious difficulty, I think,
To bring them to that prospect : Damn them then,
If ever mortal eyes do see them bolster,
More than their own ! What then ? how then ?
What shall I say ? Where's satisfaction ?
It is impossible you should see this,
Were they as prime as goats, as hot as monkeys,
As salt as wolves in pride, and fools as gross
As ignorance made drunk. But yet, I say,
If imputation, and strong circumstances,
Which lead directly to the door of truth,
Will give you satisfaction, you may have it.

OTHELLO. Give me a living reason she's disloyal.

IAGO. I do not like the office :
But, sith I am enter'd in this cause so far,—
Prick'd to it by foolish honesty and love,—

I will go on.   I lay with Cassio lately ;
And being troubled with a raging tooth,
I could not sleep.
There are a kind of men so loose of soul,
That in their sleeps will mutter their affairs,
One of this kind is Cassio.
In sleep I heard him say,—"Sweet Desdemona,
Let us be wary, let us hide our loves ! "
And then, sir, would he gripe and wring my hand,
Cry, " O sweet creature ! " and then kiss me hard,
As if he pluck'd up kisses by the roots,
That grew upon my lips : then laid his leg
Over my thigh, and sigh'd, and kissed ; and then,
Cry'd, " Cursed fate ! that gave thee to the Moor ! "

OTHELLO. O monstrous ! monstrous !

IAGO. Nay, this was but his dream.

OTHELLO. But this denoted a foregone conclusion ;
'Tis a shrewd doubt, though it be but a dream.

IAGO. And this may help to thicken other proofs,
That do demonstrate thinly.

OTHELLO.   I'll tear her all to pieces.

IAGO. Nay, but be wise ; yet we see nothing done ;
She may be honest yet.   Tell me but this,—
Have you not sometimes seen a handkerchief,
Spotted with strawberries in your wife's hand ?

OTHELLO. I gave her such a one ; 'twas my first gift.

IAGO. I know not that : but such a handkerchief,
I am sure it was your wife's, did I to-day
See Cassio wipe his beard with.

OTHELLO.   If it be that,—

IAGO. If it be that, or any that was hers,
It speaks against her with the other proofs.

OTHELLO. O, that the slave had forty thousand lives ;
One is too poor, too weak for my revenge !
Now do I see 'tis true.—Look here, Iago ;
All my fond love thus—I do blow to heaven :
'Tis gone.—

Arise, black vengeance, from thy hollow hell!
Yield up, O love, thy crown and hearted throne
To tyrannous hate! Swell, bosom, with thy fraught,
For 'tis of aspics' tongues!

IAGO. Yet, be content.

OTHELLO.   O, blood, blood, blood!

IAGO. Patience, I say; your mind, perhaps, may change.

OTHELLO. Never, Iago. Like to the Pontic sea,
Whose icy current and compulsive course
Ne'er feels retiring ebb, but keeps due on
To the Propontic, and the Hellespont;
Even so my bloody thoughts, with violent pace,
Shall ne'er look back, ne'er ebb to humble love,
Till that a capable and wide revenge
Swallow them up.—Now, by yond marble heaven,
In the due reverence of a sacred vow   [*Kneels.*]
I here engage my words.

IAGO.   Do not rise yet.   [*Kneels.*]
Witness, you ever-burning lights above!
You elements that clip us round about!
Witness, that here Iago doth give up
The execution of his wit, hands, heart,
To wrong'd Othello's service! Let him command,
And to obey shall be in me remorse,
What bloody business soever.   [*They rise.*

OTHELLO.   I greet thy love,
Not with vain thanks, but with acceptance bounteous,—
And will upon the instant put thee to't:
Within these three days let me hear thee say,
That Cassio's not alive.

IAGO. My friend is dead; 'tis done at your request:
But let her live.

OTHELLO.   Damn her, lewd minx! O, damn her!
Come, go with me apart: I will withdraw,
To furnish me with some swift means of death
For the fair devil. Now art thou my lieutenant.

IAGO. I am your own for ever.   [*Exeunt.*

BOTTOM THE WEAVER

A BUCOLIC egoist, vain, dense, and narrow.

The groundwork for this is No. 3 with a little 13 added. White is rubbed into the cheeks in the shape of high lights to broaden the appearance of the face. A triangular shadow painted on the under part of the nose makes this feature seem to tilt upward. The eyebrows are almost entirely obliterated with thick grease paint, as also are the eyelashes. The small perpendicular lines at the ends of the eyes seem to reduce their size. The corners of the mouth are extended with paint, and the tight-fitting wig drawn well over the forehead seems, while it diminishes the size of the head, to make the face appear larger.

Much of the stupidity of countenance is due to expression.

BOTTOM THE WEAVER

BOTTOM *awakes.* When my cue comes, call me, and I will answer: my next is, "Most fair Pyramus." Hey, ho! Peter Quince! Flute, the bellows-mender! Snout, the tinker! Starveling! God's, my life! stolen hence, and left me asleep. I have had a most rare vision. I have had a dream,—past the wit of man to say what dream it was. Man is but an ass, if he go about to expound this dream. Methought I was,—there is no man can tell what. Methought I was, and methought I had,—but man is but a patched fool if he will offer to say what methought I had. The eye of man hath not heard, the ear of man hath not seen, man's hand is not able to taste, his tongue to conceive, nor his heart to report, what my dream was. I will get Peter Quince to write a ballad of this dream; it shall be called Bottom's Dream, because it hath no bottom; and I will sing it in the latter end of a play, before the duke: peradventure, to make it the more gracious, I shall sing it at her death.

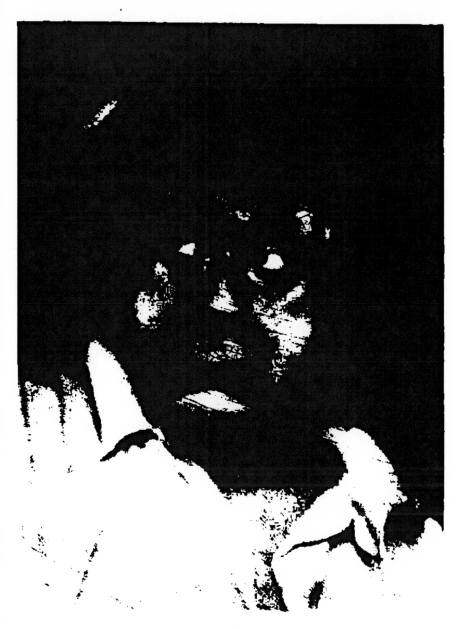

PIERROT

THE symbol of all things theatrical. The utterly impersonal medium for dramatic expression.

The mask of white destroys the distinctions of colour, race, or station. He may be emotionally, all things to all men.

Most professional clowns cover their faces with a mixture of pure oxide of zinc and lard, and then powder thickly with dry oxide of zinc. This is the method that I adopt. Some may prefer to first paint the face with white grease paint and then powder with the zinc.

The lips are painted with carmine. The eyes are outlined with black, and the eyebrows are definitely drawn. A spot of carmine is placed at the inner corner of each eye.

ROMEO

THE most romantic of the Shakespeare heroes, and physically the most attractive.

As he is a beautified edition of Hamlet, the instruction for making-up is similar. Only no effort should be made to arrive at the intellectual type of face that is striven for in the case of the more serious part.

The groundwork should be No. $2\frac{1}{2}$ with 3, a little 13, and yellow added to give it Italian warmth.

After powdering, the cheeks may be dusted with dry rouge, and this should be carried up to the temples; a little on the end of the chin is also helpful.

In juvenile make-ups it is always advisable to make the forehead lighter than the rest of the face, as it gives a feeling of animation to the countenance.

ROMEO

ROMEO. He jests at scars, that never felt a wound.

[Juliet appears above, at a window.

But, soft! what light through yonder window breaks?
It is the east, and Juliet is the sun!
Arise, fair sun, and kill the envious moon,
Who is already sick and pale with grief,
That thou, her maid, art far more fair than she
Be not her maid, since she is envious;
Her vestal livery is but sick and green,
And none but fools do wear it; cast it off.
It is my lady; O! it is my love.
O! that she knew she were!
She speaks, yet she says nothing; what of that?
Her eye discourses, I will answer it.
I am too bold, 'tis not to me she speaks:
Two of the fairest stars in all the heaven,
Having some business, do entreat her eyes
To twinkle in their spheres till they return.
What if her eyes were there, they in her head?
The brightness of her cheek would shame those stars,
As daylight doth a lamp; her eyes in heaven
Would through the airy region stream so bright,
That birds would sing, and think it were not night.
See! how she leans her cheek upon her hand!
O! that I were a glove upon that hand,
That I might touch that cheek.

THE APOTHECARY IN "ROMEO AND JULIET"

This grim compounder of death-dealing drugs was for me a most interesting part to play ; I made him up from head to foot.

From the costumier I got the oldest garments that I could procure. At the elbows, knees, and heels, I destroyed them with acid, so that when I had them on the joints protruded. The coat and cloak, if I did not carefully bind them round me, disclosed my ribs.

Wherever flesh showed I painted it in such a way that it suggested emaciation, and though in reality I am well favoured with flesh I was told that on the stage I looked like a skeleton done up in a bundle of rags.

ROMEO AND JULIET

APOTHECARY

APOTHECARY. Who calls so loud?

ROMEO. Come hither, man.   I see that thou art poor;
Hold, there is forty ducats: let me have
A dram of poison; such soon-speeding gear
As will dispense itself through all the veins,
That the life-weary taker may fall dead,
And that the trunk may be discharged of breath
As violently, as hasty powder fired
Doth hurry from the fatal cannon's womb.

APOTHECARY. Such mortal drugs I have; but Mantua's law
Is death to any he that utters them.

ROMEO. Art thou so bare, and full of wretchedness,
And fear'st to die? famine is in thy cheeks;
Need and oppression starveth in thy eyes;
Contempt and beggary, hang upon thy back,
The world is not thy friend, nor the world's law
The world affords no law to make thee rich;
Then be not poor, but break it, and take this.

APOTHECARY. My poverty, but not my will, consents.

ROMEO. I pay thy poverty, and not thy will.

APOTHECARY. Put this in any liquid thing you will,
And drink it off: and, if you had the strength
Of twenty men, it would despatch you straight.

THE THREE WITCHES IN "MACBETH"

These sub-human creatures, weird, mysterious women that seem akin to cats and bats and toads.

The first was made up by binding the nose down as is described in the instruction for Othello.

The groundwork was of No. $2\frac{1}{2}$ with a great deal of yellow and a little brown. The cheeks were deeply shadowed, as were also the cavities of the eyes. The lines running from the nostrils to the corners of the mouth were strongly defined. The form of the lips was completely obliterated. Strong shadows were painted round the mouth.

The illustration shows how definitely yellow and white were used for high lights.

For the second witch I carried my nose upward by putting a silk thread under it, which I attached to the wig. Similar groundwork was used, and the same type of shadow was placed on the cheeks and round the eyes. The teeth were partly painted out with cobblers' wax. Finely cut crepe hair was dusted on the chin.

The third witch had a nut-cracker type of nose and chin built of nose-paste. The cheeks were built out as in the case of Don Quixote.

Moles and warts were freely scattered about the lower part of the face, some of them being armed with bristles.

The colour for the groundwork and shadows was similar to that used for the first and second witches.

As I have been so frequently asked how I managed to get three photographs of myself in one print, I may explain that separate negatives were taken, which were subsequently combined in a composite print.

MACBETH

1st WITCH. Thrice the brinded cat hath mew'd.
2nd WITCH. Thrice and once the hedge-pig whin'd.
3rd WITCH. Harpier cries :—'Tis time, 'tis time.
1st WITCH. Round about the cauldron go ;
In the poison'd entrails throw.
Toad, that under cold stone,
Days and nights hast thirty-one
Swelter'd venom sleeping got,
Boil thou first i' the charmed pot !
ALL. Double, double toil and trouble ;
Fire, burn ; and, cauldron, bubble.
2nd WITCH. Fillet of a fenny snake,
In the cauldron boil and bake ;
Eye of newt, and toe of frog,
Wool of bat, and tongue of dog,
Adder's fork, and blind-worm's sting,
Lizard's leg, and owlet's wing,
For a charm of powerful trouble,
Like a hell-broth, boil and bubble.
ALL. Double, double toil and trouble ;
Fire, burn ; and, cauldron, bubble.
2nd WITCH. Cool it with a baboon's blood,
Then the charm is firm and good.

94

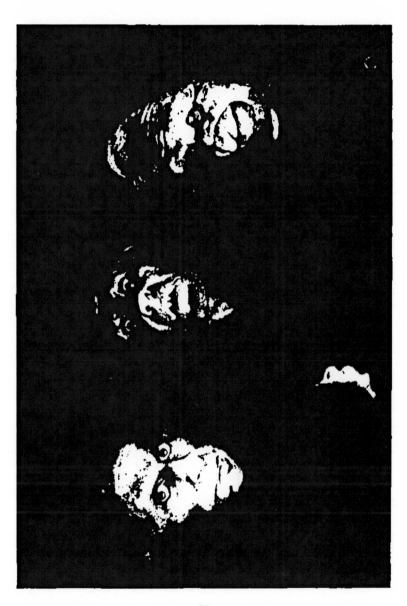

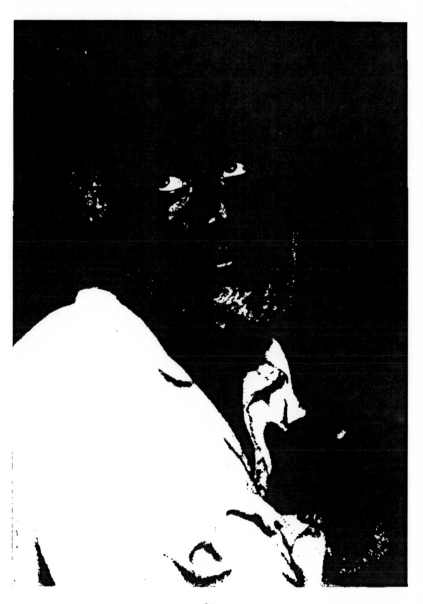

98

UNCLE TOM

This kind-hearted negro, the idol of children, devout and forbearing, has ever made a profound appeal to me.

The make-up is in many respects similar to that of Othello. In fact exactly the same instructions may be followed for shaping the nose.

The wig, beard and moustache, eyebrows and the colour of the face, give it of course an entirely different character.

The ground is of brown, with a little 13 added to give it warmth. Great care should be taken to get this colour well to the edges of the eyes or you will look more like the minstrel type of negro than that variety which was found on the plantations of Kentucky.

The hands and arms, neck and ears, should all be carefully made up.

ST. DUNSTAN

English Church Pageant, 1909.

101

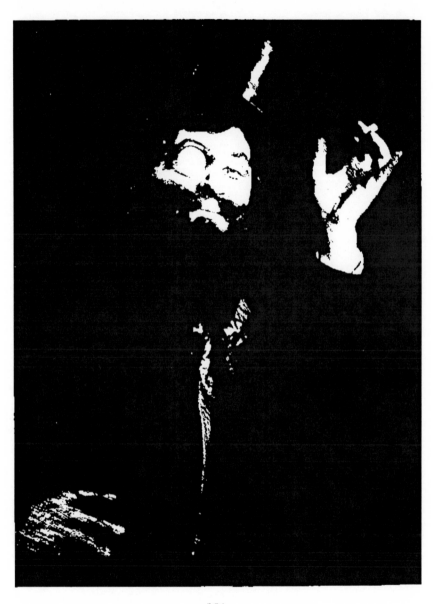

FLEURY

Gay, debauched, and lascivious.

An extreme type of French bohemian.

Notice how the moustache is brushed back from the mouth ; the insolent droop of the eyelids, and the elevation of the eyebrows.

The nose runs directly up into the forehead as in the case of Iago. The hair is long and curls in bushy masses.

Full instructions for making the beard will be found in the description accompanying the progressive stages of the false beard.

A large black-rimmed eyeglass helps the characterisation.

ABSINTHE

LINÉ. Drink ?

FLEURY. Absinthe.

LINÉ. Do you—do you—excuse me—paint ? [*Fleury shakes his head and drinks.*] You are a poet ?

FLEURY. Yes, my friend, I am [*drinks*]. I sing an answer to the siren's song. It is a ballad of such enchanting lewdness, they hold their breath to listen, and silenced they are lost. Many a dainty female thing, drunk with voluptuous ecstasy, has crept into my nets.

LINÉ. On what seas do you roam ?

FLEURY. Seas ! He that mentions water in my hearing, even if he dignifies it with the name of sea, insults me gravely. The only liquid of my life is that which but a moment since made virile this poor glass, that now alas is dead. [*Fleury's glass is filled, and he drinks, smacking his lips.*] An ocean was not too much. Nay, all the fluid systems of the world I'd gulp within. An ocean here [*putting his hand upon his stomach*], a lake upon my tongue. Through every vein a burning river run, and to my brain great clouds would rise through which pale opalescent rainbows would never cease to play.

From a Play by CAVENDISH MORTON.

THE PROFESSOR

MEN who study assiduously a certain branch of the animal kingdom sometimes grow to look more or less like the things they contemplate.

This etymologist has cultivated a family resemblance to the insects that he studies.

The inquisitive eyes and the impertinent nose might well become a mosquito.

The nose is elongated with nose-paste.

The groundwork of No. 3 is used. The shadows and wrinkles are of lake mixed with a little blue. The high lights are of pale yellow. The eyebrows are of grey made by mixing black and white paint. The eyelashes are thickly coated with white.

The face is treated with very light powder.

The spectacles, unkempt hair and velvet cap, all give characteristic touches.

Particular attention is called to the hands. They are shadowed at all spaces that occur between the bones with a mixture of lake and brown. Veins are outlined in blue and high lights on the bones and veins are accentuated with pale yellow.

THE PROFESSOR

I CAUGHT it myself. I could dance for joy. It bit me on the wrist. I watched it suck my blood. I let it quietly feed, then I put a little glass over it and held it down until it was dead.

See I have a ring upon my arm. I'll show you its sting under a microscope.

THE SOUL STRUGGLE

In this, physical expression is given to the profound spiritual conflict that takes place within a man of definitely dual personality.

He alternately comes under good and evil influences, each transition coming suddenly. As the changes occur while the character is in view of the audience, the whole effect has to be produced by the altered expression of face and of form.

When working this character up I studied the effect in a full-length mirror, striving constantly to make one character more and more dignified, while the other was persistently degraded, till, ultimately, I attained the most distinctive contrast of character that it was possible to achieve without the aid of artificial make-up.

SIR THOMAS MORE

This print is included that it may be compared with the actual Holbein print. It shows how important accuracy of detail in the costuming of a part is.

When I impersonated this character in the Chelsea Pageant, every London paper commented on the success of the make-up, the *Times* saying, if the Chancellor were to rise from the grave even he could hardly tell the difference between us; the *Standard*, that I realised Holbein's portrait with startling fidelity, and the *Daily News*, that I looked as if I had stepped directly out of Holbein's well-known canvas; while the *Sketch* and *Referee* called me a living Holbein.

SIR THOMAS MORE IN HIS GARDEN
AT CHELSEA

SIR THOMAS MORE BIDDING FAREWELL
TO HIS FAVOURITE DAUGHTER

THE additional pictures of Sir Thomas More are reproduced to show how well the illusion of character was maintained under the most trying conditions possible.

Make-up usually seems more real when seen by artificial light, but as at the Chelsea Pageant, 1908, I had no such aid, the achievement of absolute reality was all the more difficult

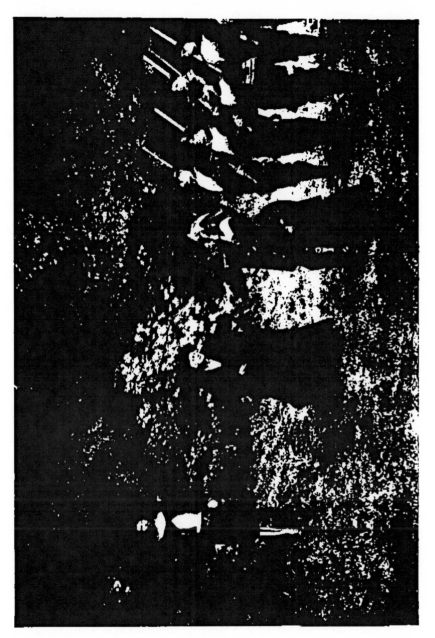

125

NAPOLEON

An example of how historical accuracy should be striven for. The success of this presentation depends on the actor more or less definitely resembling the first Emperor of the French.

In my own case the only change I had to make in my appearance was to have my hair suitably cut.

I went to infinite pains however to have each part of the costume an exact copy of that he wore.

As very few prints are seen of Napoleon in Coronation robes, perhaps the illusion will not be so striking as it would have been had I chosen to represent him wearing his well-known hat. I preferred however to represent a less hackneyed picture.

NAPOLEON

DIDEROT. I have seen him on his throne.

BARBEILLON. Was it wonderful?

DIDEROT. Wonderful! He looks like a baby swaddled in glory, sitting on his high chair.

BARBEILLON. Well?

DIDEROT. It was wonderfully pitiful and pitifully wonderful. So terribly final. There he sat like a bad boy who had stolen the toy-shop. He knows that no new thing may be created, so he sifts the old, and selecting the best puts them together as children build with blocks.

He assembles with a perfection which sickens. Triumphant arch or wedding trousseau is arranged with equal facility.

BARBEILLON. How was he dressed?

DIDEROT. The dandy of eternity, he had been to the clothing bazaar of time; taken what he fancied—Cæsar's hat, Queen Elizabeth's collar, Louis' cloak.

BARBEILLON. Extraordinary!

DIDEROT. I know; but it was all so right. Round his neck a chain, an aviary of linked golden eagles. On his breast a mighty cross of five points as if it were built to crucify the senses of the world upon. In its centre a great N, the symbol of negation to humanity. No! no! no! it said to all mankind. But I felt from the look in his eyes that it had burnt through to his own heart. He is not blazing satisfaction, only smouldering discontent.

I wonder if he'll smoulder out.

From a Play by CAVENDISH MORTON.

128

129

132

FALSE BEARDS

FALSE beards may be procured ready made on gauze, or may be made upon the face.

When a very large growth of hair is desired the wigmaker's production is most suitable, but a small beard will have a much more natural appearance if it is made up directly upon the face.

The twelve prints illustrating the method of work, practically explain themselves, but a few descriptive words may be helpful.

Crepe hair is in far too curly a condition when procured from the wigmaker, to be used with much success.

I moisten and comb out a large quantity of it, then allow it to dry.

Fig. 1 of the progressive prints shows the hair being combed out, Fig. 2 being roughly cut into shape. In Fig. 3 this piece has been gummed into position. In Fig. 4 a circular bunch has been gummed to the chin. Fig. 5 the piece under the lower lip Fig. 6 the covering of the cheek from ear to chin. Fig. 7 a small piece that runs from the corner of the mouth into the beard. Fig. 8 a blending of the beard with the cheek. Fig. 9 the placing of half the moustache. Fig. 10 the trimming of the beard. Fig. 11 illustrates how the moustache may be arranged ; and Fig. 12 that the beard may be pulled into any form.

.The hair should not be pulled out in thick masses, and when it is in position may be brushed and combed even as a real beard might. It may be trimmed into any shape with an absolute certainty of its being realistic.

137